Dear Daddy:
Remembering Him, Discovering Me

A Best-Selling Title
By Casandra Johnson

Foreword by Dr. Wanda A. Davis

Includes an Anthology of Memorable Moments and Tributes to Fathers, from the Children Who Love Them

Revised Edition

KINGDOM JOURNEY PRESS
A DIVISION OF KINGDOM JOURNEY ENTERPRISES
WOODBRIDGE, VA

Copyright Instructions
Dear Daddy: Remembering Him, Discovering Me
Copyright 2013 by Casandra Johnson
Original publication in 2008

Unless a person is explicitly identified by name, the statements that are used should not be directly attributed to any specific person.

All rights reserved under the international copyright law. No part of this book may be reproduced or transmitted in any form or by any means, electronic or mechanical, including photocopying, recording, or by any information storage and retrieval system, without the express, written permission of the author. The exception is reviewers, who may quote brief passages in a review.

Unless otherwise marked, all scripture quotations are taken from the King James Version of the Bible.

ISBN-13: 978-0-9779034-9-8

Printed in the United States of America.

Published by Kingdom Journey Press
A Division of Kingdom Journey Enterprises, Woodbridge, VA
www.kjpressinc.com

Cover Design by Brand U, Inc., www.branduinc.com

Casandra Johnson

Dedication

To every "little boy or girl" who has lost their daddy.
In honor and memory of
My daddy, Mr. Issac Johnson, Jr.

SUNRISE
February 2, 1944
Tillman, MS

-

SUNSET
October 15, 2007
Washington, DC

Aaron (Mano) Moore, Jr.
January 26, 1969 – October 27, 2008

All law enforcement officials who have been injured or killed in the line of duty (My Daddy was a Detective with the Metropolitan Police Department of Washington, DC, where he was assigned to the 3rd District. He suffered severe injuries while in the line of duty, and was medically retired in 1978.)
AND
To ALL Fathers around the world, this is a tribute to you!

Casandra Johnson

One of the Ten Commandments, as written in Exodus 20:12, tells us to

"Honor thy father and thy mother that thy days may be long upon the land which the LORD thy God giveth thee."

This is the 1st Commandment with promise!

Casandra Johnson

TABLE OF CONTENTS

ACKNOWLEDGEMENTS	xi
FOREWORD	xiii
INTRODUCTION	xix
SECTION 1 – THAT DAY	1
WHERE WERE YOU ON "THAT DAY"?	3
SUDDENLY	5
DE JA VU	7
SECTION 2 - BACK DOWN MEMORY LANE	13
A CHILD IS BORN, IN HARD TIMES MISSISSIPPI	15
THE GREAT MIGRATION – HEADED NORTH!	19
MEMORABLE MOMENTS	21
SECTION 3 – FAST FORWARD	29
GIVE HIM HIS FLOWERS	31
HONOR YOUR FATHER AND MOTHER	33
THE BOND – AS IT IS IN THE SPIRIT	35
THE GATHERING	37
THE FINAL CALL	39
"THAT DAY"	41
THE ULTIMATE CALL	45
HONORING DADDY'S FINAL REQUEST	47
NEVER WOULD HAVE MADE IT	49
SECTION 4 - A TRIBUTE TO DADDY	51
DADDY MADE THE DIFFERENCE	53
SECTION 5 – THE JOURNEY HOME	55
SECTION 6 – DEAR DADDY: AN ANTHOLOGY OF TRIBUTES, NOTES, AND MEMORABLE MOMENTS	57
DEDICATION FROM IKE JOHNSON'S LITTLE GIRLS	59
TRIBUTE TO DADDY FROM SHARON ANN BOYDE - "1ST BORN"	60
MEMORABLE MOMENTS OF A DAUGHTER GROWING UP IN THE SOUTH – LOVINGLY SUBMITTED BY RUTH HALL	61
MEMORABLE MOMENTS FROM BRENDA JENKINS	62
MEMORABLE MOMENTS OF JOHN WESLEY BARNES, SR. FROM MS. DORIS WALLS	63
A TRIBUTE TO MY FATHER BY MS. RENEE WIGGINS	64
MEMORABLE MOMENTS WITH MY FATHER BY MS. VICKIE L. EVANS	65
MY MOST MEMORABLE MOMENTS OF MY GRANDDADDY, JOHN WESLEY BARNES, SR.	66
THOUGHTS OF MY DAD – BY MS. TONYA Y. VANFIELD	67
MY MOST MEMORABLE MOMENT BY MS. DONNA COURSEY	68
MEMORABLE MOMENTS BY MS. CLAIRE TIMMS	69
TRIBUTE TO MY FATHER BY MAJOR TIMOTHY O. EVANS, USMC (RET.)	70

A TRIBUTE TO MY FATHER, JOHN WESLEY BARNES, SR. FROM LIZZIE MARIE JOHNSON.. 71
SECTION 7 - PREPARING FOR WHAT IS CERTAIN 73
APPENDIX – THE DASH 79
ABOUT THE AUTHOR 81
ABOUT KINGDOM JOURNEY PRESS 83

Casandra Johnson

Acknowledgements

First and foremost, I thank my Heavenly Father, who is The One True and Living God.

I also thank my forefathers whom I did not personally meet, and my forefathers who I did have the opportunity to meet in this life, which included my late grandfathers, Mr. Isaac Johnson, Sr. and Mr. John Wesley Barnes, Sr. and my late father, Mr. Issac Johnson, Jr.

A special thanks to my family and everyone who has prayed, stood by, and supported me throughout this Kingdom Journey: My mother, Lizzie Johnson, my two sisters Sharon and Stephanie, and my nieces and nephews. My late grandmother, Mrs. Julia M. Johnson, who passed away as the manuscript for this book was being completed. She always encouraged me to keep trusting God and to write. I am thankful to God for allowing me to place the initial version of "Dear Daddy" into her hands prior to her passing. Uncle John, (the "Jr." from my mother's side of the family) who also passed away as "Dear Daddy:" was being published. Thanks for being there on "that day" to tell me it would be ok. I pray you smiled as God allowed me to tell your children the same thing as they too experienced "that day" just a few months later.

Last, but certainly not least, my baby girl – Brittany, an anointed young woman of God! We made it through another day's journey and it was nobody but God who kept us. Our latter days shall be greater than the former days!

Casandra Johnson

FOREWORD

While this is probably one of the most painful endorsements, it is also one of the most necessary endorsements. I salute Casandra Johnson's latest literary project, "Dear Daddy". I know only too well the value of a good, Godly father who not only fathered me in the natural, but also led me to know and love my Heavenly Father, the Lord Jesus Christ. My father, Bishop Lewis D. Stallworth of Stockton, CA just passed a few months ago…and the pain is fresh. The pain is real…the pain is deep! That's because the life of a Godly father based on God's original blueprint for the family…is so dear and valuable. Thanks Casandra for the photograph of what a good father, a Godly father and biblical family looks like. I lived it, you wrote it.

Dr. Wanda A. Davis, minister, counselor and writer

Casandra Johnson

For years, Father's Day has often been viewed by many as just another day – often going unrecognized and under celebrated. The mere utter of the words "Daddy" or "Father" have had a tendency to stir up varying degrees of thoughts and emotions due to the overwhelming number of strained family relationships resulting from families that have been torn apart by separation, divorce, and out-of-wedlock pregnancies, where most often, the mother has been left alone to raise the children who were born out of these relationships. Even in instances where fathers were in the home, often times, he was often still "absent" due to his role as the provider which often calls for long work hours and various other commitments outside of the home.

"Dear Daddy" is written and designed to serve as a roadmap to restore and ignite bonds between fathers and children, and help families begin the journey of creating strong relationships that will last a lifetime and carry forward into future generations.

Enjoy the Journey!

Casandra Johnson

Behold, I will send you Elijah the prophet before the coming of the great and dreadful day of the LORD: And he shall turn the heart of the fathers to the children, and the heart of the children to their fathers, lest I come and smite the earth with a curse.

Malachi 4:5-6

Casandra Johnson

INTRODUCTION

One of the Ten Commandments, as written in Exodus 20:12 tells us to "Honor thy father and thy mother that thy days may be long upon the land with the LORD thy God giveth thee." This is the first Commandment with promise!

"Dear Daddy:" is a tribute to fathers and documents what in fact is far from uncommon in today's society. You see, mama and daddy separated and divorced when their three children were very young. This resulted in mama being forced to take on two roles to not only be mama, but also to try to fill the role of daddy, which is one I am certain God never intended, nor one which she desired. Although we experienced a lot of difficult while growing up, we still somehow managed to develop a bond with daddy, in spite of the adverse circumstances; one that could not be broken or destroyed, even when faced with one of the most difficult challenges of our lives - the loss of daddy.

"Dear Daddy:" is a story of love, pain, joy, sorrow, forgiveness, and ultimate healing that would result in the dawning of a new day. You are invited to share the trials and triumphs of not only this family, but also be inspired by an anthology of tributes, notes and memorable moments from several others.

For some reading this book, perhaps daddy is gone, and what remains are the memories of words spoken and special moments while he was here on Earth.

For others, daddy is still alive, but may or may not have been in the home.

Whatever the case may have been for you as a child and even stemming forward into adulthood, "Dear Daddy" is designed to prompt and stimulate healthy relationships and memorable moments which will allow you to develop a greater love for self, those you are connected to, including fathers if at all possible, but most importantly with your Heavenly Father.

Some of the notes, tributes and memorable moments shared in "Dear Daddy" have been previously communicated; however others are being made available for the very first time ever.

Casandra Johnson

Section 1 – That Day

Casandra Johnson

… Section 1 – That Day

WHERE WERE YOU ON "THAT DAY"?

There are some moments in time that will forever remain embedded in one's memory, just as if it were yesterday. These are moments in history where many are able to recall exactly where they were or what they were doing when the event occurred. Like on the following days:

November 22, 1963 when President John F. Kennedy was assassinated.
Or
April 4, 1968 when Dr. Martin Luther King, Jr. was assassinated.

While both of these events occurred prior to my birth, the moments in history which stand out in my memory are:

January 28, 1986 when the Challenger Space Shuttle exploded.
And
September 11, 2001 when terrorists used airplanes to crash into the Twin Towers at the World Trade Center in New York, NY, the Pentagon in Arlington, VA, and a field in Somerset County, PA.

In each instance, the lives of fathers, and others, were tragically ended.

While I can recall exactly where I was and what I was doing when the latter two events occurred, the moment in time that would become the most personal for me was October 15, 2007, shortly after 4:22 in the morning. On "that day," my life was forever changed.

Casandra Johnson

Section 1 – That Day

SUDDENLY

Have you ever had a "suddenly" moment that has caused your life to be forever changed?

In an instant, with no plans or expectations, the unimaginable happens, "suddenly".

Something so devastating, heart wrenching, irreversible - occurs, "suddenly".

During one moment, everything appears OK, and then out of nowhere, there is a sudden turn of events – the type of event which causes many to begin viewing life and relationships from a totally different perspective.

You see, my daddy did not live in the home with his children as they were growing up. Mama and Daddy divorced when their children were small, so needless to say, our family did not have the "ideal" household experience - no Huxtable family here!

Maybe you grew up having daddy in the home and were able to experience the "ideal" upbringing. Or maybe even though daddy was present in the home, there were still memorable moments that you longed to create.

Perhaps daddy was not in the home, which unfortunately is the case for so many "little sons and daughters." As a result, daddy's absence created a strained relationship where "something" was missing. This "something" resulted in a longing and desire for the love, bond and affirmation that only daddy could provide.

Maybe daddy mailed a card, and what you truly desired was a call or visit. Maybe there were missing words, such as "I Love You," or "Thank You," or "I'm Sorry," or "Forgive Me," or "I Need You," or "I Miss You," or "You Are Beautiful," or "Let's go to lunch or dinner," or "Congratulations," or "You Can Do It!" or "Happy Birthday," or "Merry Christmas," or "I Believe in YOU!"

For many, daddy was far from what we desired for him to be as a father.

As I grew into adulthood and began to develop a stronger relationship with my Heavenly Father, I would come to learn and gain a greater understanding of the relationship that God designed for families, which included fathers. I also realized the importance of understanding him in order to discover me, with a realization that perhaps it was the breach in our relationship that brought about so many struggles for me in developing relationships with others.

What I later realized was I was longing for the special love and nurturing that was reserved for daddy to give me as his child. In trying to understand what may have been plaguing his soul, it was also just important to reach back to prior generations to understand what may have very well been inherited from past struggles, hurts and pain from my forefathers. Without this understanding, it has the potential to positively or negatively mold and shape our patterns and behaviors, unknowingly, which can result in self-inflicted hurt not only to ourselves, but also to others.

With this new found level of understanding, a bond was developed some years later between daddy and his children, in spite of the fact of us growing up under adverse circumstances. And it seemed like just as quickly as it happened, daddy was gone. And it happened suddenly!

DE JA VU

Daddy was one of Washington, DC's finest during the 1970s, assigned to the 3rd District as a Detective. The very nature of his job caused his life to be on the line each time he suited up for duty.

After only a few years of active service on the force, daddy experienced one of those "suddenly" moments where he sustained a severe injury as a result of a heroic act to protect his partner. It was a courageous move which prevented what could have been a deadly blow. In spite of the pain daddy continued to experience for the rest of his life, he still ended up being "ok", however he was forced into early retirement.

And just as a phone call was received on "that day," this same family would be faced with another near tragic event a few years earlier, where the series of events were very similar.

Dreams and Visions

And it shall come to pass afterward, that I will pour out my spirit upon all flesh; and your sons and your sons and your daughters shall prophesy, your old men shall dream dreams, your young men shall see visions: Joel 2:28

In 1990 while I was away in the military, I had a dream. In the dream, I received a phone call from my mother stating that my father had been in a car accident and had died as a result of the injuries. I was far away from home and was devastated.

While my father and I had a relationship to some degree as I was growing up, it was strained, even to the extent that he was not pleased about my decision to join the military. What he did not know was I was also having my own private struggles about being there. When I was a senior in high school, I had taken the time to apply to Howard University and even paid the application fee on my own. I received an acceptance letter, however I did not share it with either of my parents because I did not think we had the money for me to attend. As a result, I believed it was a hopeless dream. Not knowing what to do with my life after high school, I knew I had to do something, which resulted in my decision to go into the Marine Corps. I have now come to realize that just The Bible tells us in Romans 8:28, "And we know that all things work together for good to them that love God, to them who are the called according to His purpose." Today, I am at peace with my decision and there have been a lot of rewards that resulted from it.

Anyway, back to the dream. It seemed so real to me. When I woke up, I earnestly prayed for God to keep my father here on Earth. I was only 21 at the time, and was still longing for a closer relationship with my father. I realized that I longed for something only daddy could provide. I called mama and asked her to pray with me. In spite of the flaws we both possessed, I was a part of him and he was a part of me.

Some years later, I had another dream. In this particular dream, my sister called and stated that her two sons had been shot and were killed instantly. Once again, the dream startled me because it seemed so real. When I woke from the dream, I immediately called my sister and shared the dream. We agreed that we had to trust God to protect them because the reality was there were so many young black males being murdered I our nation due to senseless street violence.

In both instances, God allowed there to be advanced warning, thereby alerting us to pray. As stated in James 5:16, "The effectual fervent prayer of a righteous man availeth much.

We've Been Here Before

On one clear Saturday evening, gunshots were sprayed into the car daddy had given to his eldest grandson. It was an older model vehicle, made with steel, unlike the cars today. The older brother, who was driving, saw the bullets coming and ducked just in the nick of time. He would cheat death as a result of a bullet that could have pierced through his heart. Instead, the bullet hit the metal frame of the car's seat. Because of the steel frame in the seats, the bullet should have ricocheted and come back forward, hitting him in the back, however it shifted and exited the car through the driver's side door.

The younger brother, who was riding on the passenger's side, and one of the passengers in the back seat were not as fortunate. What was once intended as an evening of fun for four teenagers turned into a ride for their lives.

As they raced in the direction of the nearest hospital, based on directions that were being provided by the brother who had been hit, they called 9-1-1. A subsequent and frantic call was also made to their mom, who in turn made an attempt to notify mama. She was unable to get through on mama's phone line so she called my cell phone instead.

She said "I need to speak to mama." She began providing the details of the shooting and then said "they are being rushed to the hospital."

Once the conversation began to register, my mind instantly went back to the dream. What came to mind however was one detail that was different from the dream – the report was they were being rushed to the hospital, versus them dying instantly, like in the dream. At that point, I received comfort in knowing God was working it out and he plans the enemy had to kill them had been thwarted.

A few moments after the local hospital was put on alert, their car came speeding into the emergency room driveway! Their mom also came racing to the

Section 1 – That Day

hospital, which was only a few minutes away from where she lived. When she first arrived, she was told that her son was fine and had only been hit in his arm by a bullet. On the other hand, his best friend was seriously injured and needed immediate medical attention. As she was praying for his best friend and desperately trying to reach his mother, a doctor approached her and advised that it was not the best friend, but actually her son who was fighting for his life.

After a quick evaluation and assurance that there was health insurance coverage, the hospital staff made a determination that this case was too much for them to handle. As a result, in comes the med-evac helicopter to take him on another ride for his life. As he is being air-lifted to the nearest shock trauma unit, phone calls went out to the rest of the immediate family, who set in motion to respond accordingly. We continued calling on The God of our salvation, and then headed to the hospital during the wee hours of the morning, each driving from different locations, at what later seemed like the speed of lightning on a major interstate that's known across the country for carrying one of the heaviest loads of traffic on a daily basis. On this particular morning however, the highways were clear as God's angels guided each car to the same destination. We all arrived within a few minutes of each other not sure what to expect. As we came together, we began asking questions to ourselves and aloud, like:

"Is he OK?"

"Who did it?"

"How did this happen?"

"What really happened?

"Why?"

We sat, waiting, until we heard the sounds of the med-evac helicopter, preparing for landing. We stood watching as the technicians brought our loved one's motionless body into the hospital. The doctors and staff quickly came to his aid to conduct an evaluation. Shortly thereafter, the doctor came to address our family, informing us that there was a bullet lodged at the roof of his mouth. The doctor went on to say "There is extensive damage, but he will be ok."

We rejoiced for the great news!

What we did not know however was the worst had not yet occurred. As my nephew lay in a motionless state for several hours, heavily sedated, the bullet traveled and eventually became lodged between his spinal cord and the main artery in the back of his neck. The same doctor had to come back to the waiting area to give an updated, grim report. He notified us that there was a need for emergency surgery to remove the bullet. He also told us that because of where the bullet was now lodged, there was a strong chance that he could bleed to death during the surgery. On the other hand, while the surgery was very risky and dangerous, he could also die without it.

As we stood together in the waiting room of one of the nation's leading hospitals, all we could do was continue to trust God and begin to pray Psalms 91:

> [1]*He that dwelleth in the secret place of the most High shall abide under the shadow of the Almighty.*
>
> [2]*I will say of the LORD, He is my refuge and my fortress: my God; in him will I trust.*
>
> [3]*Surely he shall deliver thee from the snare of the fowler, and from the noisome pestilence.*
>
> [4]*He shall cover thee with his feathers, and under his wings shalt thou trust: his truth shall be thy shield and buckler.*
>
> [5]*Thou shalt not be afraid for the terror by night; nor for the arrow that flieth by day;*
>
> [6]*Nor for the pestilence that walketh in darkness; nor for the destruction that wasteth at noonday.*
>
> [7]*A thousand shall fall at thy side, and ten thousand at thy right hand; but it shall not come nigh thee.*
>
> [8]*Only with thine eyes shalt thou behold and see the reward of the wicked.*
>
> [9]*Because thou hast made the LORD, which is my refuge, even the most High, thy habitation;*
>
> [10]*There shall no evil befall thee, neither shall any plague come nigh thy dwelling.*
>
> [11]*For he shall give his angels charge over thee, to keep thee in all thy ways.*
>
> [12]*They shall bear thee up in their hands, lest thou dash thy foot against a stone.*
>
> [13]*Thou shalt tread upon the lion and adder: the young lion and the dragon shalt thou trample under feet.*
>
> [14]*Because he hath set his love upon me, therefore will I deliver him: I will set him on high, because he hath known my name.*
>
> [15]*He shall call upon me, and I will answer him: I will be with him in trouble; I will deliver him, and honour him.*

Section 1 – That Day

¹⁶With long life will I satisfy him, and shew him my salvation.

After being in surgery for several hours, the chief surgeon returned to the waiting room to address the family. With a serious look on his face, he staged "This was in fact one of the most difficult surgeries of my entire career. And then with a smile on his face, he said "but he survived!"

As the entire family all stood together on one accord, we rejoiced and thanked the God of our salvation for answering our prayers during one of our most difficult storms, ever.

It was a miracle surgery!

It took a few days for him to recover and begin eating – three days to be exact! Different family members rotated shifts at the household around the clock. Today, he has fully recovered from the injuries, with only a tiny scar on the cheek which is not visibly noticeable. We held onto the memories of God's grace and mercy in sparing his life. God stepped in to prevent us from experiencing a tragic, sudden loss of our 17 year old loved one, who later shared that he could hear Psalms 91 being read to him while lying in an unconscious state.

For so many families, this is not always the outcome. Unfortunately, there have been an overwhelming number of young lives snuffed out across the nation due to senseless street violence. Today, we acknowledge and pray for families that have lost loved ones. We also salute DC's finest and all law enforcement officials who put their lives on the line in an effort to combat street violence, just as daddy did.

And just as a similar series of events would begin to unfold on "that day," it appeared to us that we had been "here" before!

Casandra Johnson

Section 2 - Back Down Memory Lane

Casandra Johnson

A Child Is Born, In Hard Times Mississippi

February 2nd, 1944 - Tillman, MS was the place.

A child, Isaac (Ike) Johnson, Jr., is born during an era of segregation, discrimination and the days where many blacks in the south worked in cotton fields.

His family would later move from Tillman to Port Gibson, MS, with the assistance of Mr. John Wesley Barnes – who was mama's daddy. Several families became connected and raised their children together - The Johnson's, the Barnes', the Walls', the Nelson's, the Gibson's, the Landers', the Banks', the Wilson's, the Leasly's, the Giles', the Odoms', and many others.

Some of Port Gibson's key landmarks were Ms. Bessie Weathers' Store, The Juke Joint, The Blue Hole, Addison High School, Alcorn State University, "Town," Piggly Wiggly, Jitney Jungle, and Fort Gibson.

As years went by, a love story developed between "Ike" from the Johnson family and "Liz" from the Barnes family. They both attended Addison High, where Ike played football and Liz was a cheerleader. Each of their siblings also participated in various forms of sports and school activities. As this story continued to unfold, there were a series of double dates between Ike Johnson and Liz Barnes, and Liz's sister Rosa Barnes and her high school sweetheart.

After graduation, Ike enlisted in the U.S. Army and left for basic training in 1963. During the same year, Liz's family moved to Gulfport, MS, located on the gulf coast, close to four hours away from Port Gibson. This was also the same year President John F. Kennedy was assassinated.

The move for the Barnes family was not by choice however, but by force. You see, granddaddy was considered to be one of the wealthier blacks in the Port Gibson area during that era. To make matters worse, he was also very active in the civil rights movement. As a result of the times, many did not like what granddaddy was doing, therefore he was often threatened, and ultimately forced out of town, leaving behind all of his property. A few years prior to grandma's passing in 1981, she revealed that granddaddy, or Bro John as he was affectionately known, had been told that if he didn't get out of town as quickly as possible, then the entire family would be killed. While granddaddy did not want to move away, he decided to leave town at the urging of grandma and for the love of his family.

As daddy would go into the army, and mama's family would make this major transition from Port Gibson to Gulfport, it would also be the same year of the assassination of President John F. Kennedy. During Ike's military career, his duty stations would include Germany and Texas. He was later discharged from the Army in 1967. In spite of the separation and distance, it would not stop Ike and Liz. As a result of their union, three little girls were born as:

Sharon Ann Johnson, July 27, 1964 in Gulfport, MS;

Casandra Denise Johnson, April 11, 1969 in Gulfport, MS;

Stephanie Lynette Johnson, August 10, 1972 in Washington, DC.

Section 2 - Back Down Memory Lane

Fill in the blanks to provide information about your parents and siblings

Daddy's Name:

Date of Birth:

Place of Birth:

Mama's Name:

Date of Birth:

Place of Birth:

1st Born:

Date of Birth:

Place of Birth:

2nd Born:

Date of Birth:

Place of Birth:

3rd Born:

Date of Birth:

Place of Birth:

4th Born:

Date of Birth:

Place of Birth:

If there are more than four siblings, feel free to include all additional names and information.

Casandra Johnson

THE GREAT MIGRATION – HEADED NORTH!

Because of the environment and harsh treatment that African-Americans were subjected to in the south, Ike had no desire to live in Mississippi after being discharged from the Army. As a result, he, mama, and their first born child would head north to the big city - Washington, DC!

The time was March 1968. One of Liz's older sisters and her husband were already living in the big city. Upon arrival, Ike, Liz, and their first born child would stay with them for about a month, until they could get established. Liz's brother-in-law, who also attended high school with them in Port Gibson, was working for one of the city's landmark establishments - Woodward and Lothrop, also known as Woodies. Soon after their arrival, Ike would also get a job at Woodies at the downtown, DC location on 10th and F Street NW. This put Ike and Liz in a position to get their own place in the Southeast section of Washington, DC – just minutes away from Bolling AFB and Downtown DC!

"Wow, they were in Washington, DC!" They were living for the city!!!!

It was time for them to begin building a better life - one different from what they once knew in the south. They were now in a land that offered great promise and opportunities for African-Americans. Their move north would be a continuation from "the great migration," a time where millions of Blacks moved from the southern United States to cities in the North, Midwest and West. Just as daddy and mama came to the big city for a new start, several of their other family members and childhood friends would also follow. As had been the case with daddy and mama, they would also provide a temporary place to aid family members with getting a new start; it was a given.

Shortly after Ike and Liz's move to the big city, news of the assassination of Dr. Martin Luther King, Jr. on April 4, 1968 would swiftly circulate around the country. Ike and Liz would find themselves living in the big city on "that day" as riots would break out in Washington, DC and other major cities around the country. Many of the streets and business establishments were literally destroyed. Although this was a new environment for them and a difficult time for almost everyone around the country, mama and daddy stayed in DC!

I was born in 1969, one year after my parent's move to the big city. By this time, they had become settled in Washington, DC. Mama returned home to Gulfport for my delivery however. It was the same year as Hurricane Camille - one of the worst hurricanes to ever hit the Gulf Coast and United States - at least until Hurricane Katrina came on the scene 36 years later! Shortly after my delivery, mama would return to DC, with a new little baby in tow.

Several years later, after their 3rd and youngest daughter was born in 1972, mama and daddy would separate and ultimately divorce, thus starting a new era. Daddy and mama were once again at a point of decision as it related to remaining in the big city. They both decided to stay and make Washington, DC their home!

… Section 2 - Back Down Memory Lane

MEMORABLE MOMENTS

What our family experienced is one of the unfortunate results that so often occur with divorce. The separation commonly leads to broken family relationships, where the children often do not establish a strong relationship with the family members of the parent who is not in the home. In spite of the situation for our family, we were however able to capture some very fond memories as some of daddy's family members came to DC to visit or also explored the option of moving to the big city.

Daddy's Family

I can recall an occasion in the early 70's where one of daddy's younger brothers came to stay for an extended period. At that time, we lived in an apartment in the Southwest section of Washington, DC, off of Martin Luther King, Jr. Ave.

My uncle had gotten a job at the McDonald's that was in Oxon Hill, MD, which was only a few minutes away and just across the DC border. One day after working the closing shift, he walked home, as he often did, to find that no one was home. He left and came back later, which was close to 3:00 in the morning. He asked daddy and mama where they were when he came home the first time.

"At a party," they replied. The children had been with daddy's sister, who lived just one street over.

My uncle's response was "People in Mississippi are in the bed at this time of mornin'."

I was a very little girl then – maybe about three years old. I can clearly remember as if it were yesterday, just looking up at him with a deep stare.

Because I would not stop looking, he asked, "What you lookin' at me for Ca-saaaaan-dra?"

This was in fact one of my most fondest and memorable moments of daddy's family members.

They're Home

The day that mama and daddy brought my youngest sister home for the first time was something special! It was probably 2-3 days after she was born. During those times, mothers and their newborn babies would stay in the hospital for a few days even after a normal delivery, which is unlike today. I remember anxiously looking out the living room window of our 3rd floor apartment with great excitement about having a new sibling. I stood there, watching as the little white Volkswagen pulled up in front of our building on the opposite side of the street. I was only three years old, but so excited about now being a big sister. Sadly enough, this was really the last clear memory that I have of daddy being in the home. It seems like shortly thereafter, he was gone.

Family Dinners During the Holidays

And I remember families coming together for holiday dinners, even in the big city, just as we continued to do after the divorce. The adults would all sit around and talk and laugh about the good old times from when they were growing up in Mississippi. The children would often get to listen in, unless we were off having our own fun!

I recently moved to Atlanta, where I go almost daily to one of the local walking paths for morning exercise. During these special moments, I often meet up with several groups of older people who are out for their morning walk. As I have the opportunity to speak and also listen to many of them, it serves as a reminder of how it used to be "back in the day." Many of them are like pillars in the community, or "Legends" as Oprah would call them. As a matter of fact, one of the walkers that I have met up with on several occasions was a key participant at Oprah's Legends Ball.

The walkers are often out strolling, and reminiscing about memorable moments and the times when "Dr. King was alive." Perhaps, maybe this is part of what it has meant for me to be in Atlanta - a reminder of the way it used to be when the older people would speak, and the younger generation would listen and learn. It allowed us to continue a legacy from the stories that they would share.

DC'S Finest

Shortly after arriving in Washington, DC and after a brief stint of working at Woodies, daddy was accepted into the Police Academy. Upon successful completion of the rigorous training, he graduated in 1970.

When daddy's girls were younger, to us, it was as if "everybody" knew him.

Of course everyone knew him because he was one of DC's finest!

Daddy would take his little girls to what seemed like everywhere and little did we know, "everybody" knew us too. He was always taking us around his police buddies and their families for food, fun, and fellowship. Wow, we were all living for the city, in Washington, DC!!

The Weather Report

After daddy was medically retired from the force, we learned that he would become an "unofficial" meteorologist, having the ability to predict when a storm was coming.

You see on one dreadful evening, daddy's partner on the police force made an arrest. The suspect had to be taken in for booking, in handcuffs of course. As daddy's partner turned his back to file the reports, the suspect would pick up a

Section 2 - Back Down Memory Lane

chair, attempting to hit him in the head - a blow that could have been fatal! Daddy, being the person that he was, jumped in the way of his partner and took a serious blow to his shoulder. As a result of this injury, daddy's active career as one of DC's finest came to an end.

So now that daddy was no longer an active police officer, the little girls were now able to go to his house more often on the weekends. Daddy now lived in the Fort Totten section of Northeast Washington, DC. Daddy would come to pick us up in his white Volkswagen, or a 2nd car that he later purchased, which was a Cutlass Supreme. We would go from Oxon Hill, MD to the Fort Totten section of DC to hang out with him and his roommate, who was also one of DC's finest.

Upon notification that daddy was coming, the three little girls would get excited about what they knew would often be a visit to McDonald's. Perhaps we were drawn in by their slogan at that time, "At McDonald's, we do it all for you", or the signs posted under the golden arches stating "over 1 million hamburgers served!" or obviously, their famous fries.

Our trips to McDonald's normally occurred on the first night of our visit as we would be enroute to daddy's house. On many occasions, we would stop at the McDonalds at the intersection of New York Avenue and Florida Avenue in the Northeast section of DC, just a few blocks over from North Capitol Street. We typically would each get a hamburger, fries, and orange soda, which was before the days of Happy Meals. It was the bomb! Of course it was because back then, going to McDonald's was considered as a treat and not a way of life. It was one of the highlights of our weekend and daddy's little girls were SATISFIED!!!

But of course, our weekend activities all depended on the weather report, which there were many weekends where the weather prevented us from going out. You see, when there was going to be a bad storm, daddy would know in advance. If rain was coming, he would begin to experience excruciating pain in his shoulder, which meant that we were not going to be able to go anywhere. And guess what, when he said it was going to rain, it would actually rain just like he predicted. So on those days, we would hang out in the house and play cards or watch TV, and often eat crabs during the summer months. When we did get to out however, it was all the way live! We would go to places such as his friends' houses, or different restaurants in the DC area like Shakey's Pizza.

Our dinner outings would always be quite funny and eventful! We would sit at the table, place our order, and from there, it was on - let the fun begin! Daddy would always joke with the servers, other guests in the restaurant, and with us.

Whenever we went out to eat, there was always one ritual that we maintained, which was this:

As we were close to finishing our meal, daddy would say, ok, I'm going to the bathroom. He would tell us, after I'm gone for a couple minutes, then Sharon, you go to the bathroom, and then Casandra was to follow next, leaving the youngest sister, Stephanie, who he would tell to leave last. The plan was that if the server came back before Stephanie could leave, then most likely they would feel sorry for her and just let her go because she was little. It was always the same joke, but we would get a kick out of it every time. After he would give us the instructions, he would say, ok, we won't do it this time because if we leave, the police will get us and take us to jail, and we certainly didn't want to go to jail! Remember, daddy was once one of DC's finest and perhaps this was a type of call that he often encountered while on the force.

Weathering The Storm

I remember when mama had to go into the hospital for an operation. It was in 1973, which means that I was only about four years old. By this time, mama and daddy had separated. We were still living in the same apartment building in the Southwest section of Washington, DC, which is no longer there. While we knew at the time that mama was in the hospital, it would not be until years later that we learned how serious it was and that she almost died. Mama later shared that at one point, she had to be put on a bed of ice because of an infection that set in, causing her to have an extremely high fever.

While mama was in the hospital, daddy and some of their very close friends took care of their three little girls. On one of the nights, it started snowing really bad. This was a night that daddy had to go to work and we were scheduled to stay at the friends' home. They were once our neighbors on Danbury Street, but by this time, they had moved to the suburbs in Prince George's County in an area called Oxon Run. It was not very far from where we lived, but certainly not within normal walking distance.

As the snow started falling, daddy proceeded to take us to the friend's home in the white Volkswagen. By the time we arrived at their house, the snow had gotten really bad. Daddy was committed to going to work on that evening, just as he was on "that day." As he left to prepare to go to work, he got to a point where he could not drive any further, causing the car to become stuck. As you know, there were no cell phones at this time. As a result, daddy ended up having to leave the Volkswagen parked on the street and walking all the way back to our house. On that night, he weathered the storm, but needless to say, he ended up not making it to work.

The Bus Rides Uptown

I'm not quite sure when it all started, but I believe it was on an occasion when daddy was down to only one car, which wasn't working and it was on a weekend when we were scheduled to go to daddy's house.

So with no transportation, what were we to do? Mama didn't drive, which

Section 2 - Back Down Memory Lane

meant that we had become accustomed to getting around the city on the Metrobus. As children, we learned how to ride the bus to most places around the city, and we got around with no problem. As a young child, I actually knew how to ride the bus just about anywhere around the city, by myself. This was of course during the late 70s and early 80s, before the serious crime wave hit DC.

By this time, we had moved to Prince Georges County in Oxon Hill, MD, just minutes away from the DC line. When we needed to go into the city, we had a choice of either catching a bus from our community to the district line in Southeast DC, which would have cost an additional fare, or we could walk since it was only a short distance. By going to the DC line, we could gain access to more bus routes, which also ran more frequently. The metro buses in DC would actually run throughout the night, which was not the case in Maryland.

With the dilemma of daddy's car not working, we decided to hit the bus to go from Southeast DC to the other side of town to Northeast DC, with mama's concurrence of course. After about two to three bus transfers, which equated to about two hours, we ended up at our final destination - the Fort Totten section of Washington, DC.

We had so much fun! What we learned was there were card games which occurred on some of the buses, particularly along the routes that traveled down North Capital Street. There were people that would strategically plan the bus routes and keep card games going throughout the duration of the route.

As a result of this day, something happened that would change our desires for how we would travel to daddy's house. With this new found excitement, we decided from that point forward that we didn't need a car to go to visit daddy, but the Metrobus was our way to go. We would tell daddy not to come get us, but to just look out for us at a certain time, as we were able to time our trip depending on when we departed from Oxon Hill. Daddy's little girls had the plan. Some Fridays would be an early arrival and others would be late in the evenings. And on most trips, we would catch a card game. We were now living for the city too, and we loved it!

Our Last Time Eating Out Together

Daddy and I were supposed to meet for dinner on Father's Day in 2007. It never happened however due to very difficult situation that occurred in our family around the same time.

The last time that we actually met to eat at a restaurant was April 2007 at the Boulevard at the Capital Centre in Maryland. I remember having my mind set on Gladys and Ron's Chicken and Waffles. On that day, I wanted their salmon and vegetables.

Daddy only lived a few minutes away from the location, however I was traveling from Virginia, which was close to a 45 minute drive, without traffic.

Casandra Johnson

When we spoke as I was leaving, daddy told me to call him again as I was getting close to the area. When I called him back, he told me that he wanted to go to Golden Corral's. While I was a little disappointed because my taste buds were set for Gladys and Ron's, I graciously agreed.

What I did not know was that I would have to sit in the parking lot once I arrived and wait for daddy for close to an hour. Remember, daddy only lived a few minutes away and I was the one who had to drive for almost an hour. When daddy finally arrived, he came to the table with a big smile on his face, just like it was no big deal. By that time, I had already started to eat because I had to get back to Virginia to pick up a group of students from school. Daddy shared that he was on his way, but had to stop and talk to one of the neighbors about their lawn. While it wasn't funny while I was waiting in the parking lot for almost an hour, all I could do was laugh.

So once again, we laughed for a while, ate, and eventually I would have to leave daddy as he finished up his meal. It proved to be a special and enjoyable day for both of us. Unlike our ritual during my childhood days, on this occasion, I had to leave first. We didn't have the opportunity to consider the plan because our meals were already paid for as a result of Golden Corral's advance payment policy.

Section 2 - Back Down Memory Lane

What are some of your most memorable childhood moments?

Who:

What:

When:

Where:

How:

Casandra Johnson

What are some of your most memorable childhood moments with daddy?

Restaurant
Birthday
Holiday
Movie
Food
Car
School moment
Conversation
Father's Day

Section 3 – Fast Forward

Section 3 – Fast Forward

GIVE HIM HIS FLOWERS

It is so often said to give "her" flowers while she can smell them. As Mother's Day arrives every year, florist shops are inundated with orders and their prices are normally increased substantially. This is certainly understandable as most mothers go over and above to provide unconditional love and care for their children, just as our mama did. As a result, most mothers are celebrated not only on Mother's Day, but throughout the year. This is something that my sisters and I have done for our mama over the years and because we are fortunate to have her still with us, it's something that we continue to do to this day. With the relationship that I have personally developed with mama, there is not a day that goes by that we don't speak to each other on the phone.

Such is not the case for many fathers. On one Father's Day, I wondered what I could do different for daddy. In years past, I would send cards or we would often get together for dinner, plus I was also known for getting him the latest cologne for Christmas, birthdays, or Father's Day. I would go to the men's cologne counter at major department stores and request the best of the best, the latest and fresh for my daddy.

On this particular Father's Day, I wanted to do something different and special. So I went on-line and ordered flowers for my daddy. Because it was Father's Day and it was not the norm for sales to skyrocket, I was able to place a last minute order that was delivered on time, and also pay normal price. Because it's not typical to give flowers to men, I wanted to send an arrangement that would be fitting for my daddy and something that I thought daddy would like. I wanted to send him the best and most beautiful arrangement, so that's what I did.

I will never forget when the phone rang and it was daddy on the other end. He was literally in tears when he called. He shared that when he received the flowers, that he was overwhelmed and overjoyed because he had never received flowers. Prior to that, I had not even thought about the fact that daddy owned a landscaping business, which he loved and had a tremendous passion for. He was accustomed to doing lawns and flowers for others, and even did it for his little girls, but how often would he receive his own flowers? It was a moment that I will never forget.

We followed up with dinner - Outback Steakhouse was his choice, so that's where we went. On this day, it was daddy and his two younger daughters. We experienced a little wait, as many other families were also taking their daddy out to dinner for Father's Day. We laughed, talked about the old times, and even reminisced about our old ritual from when he would take us out to eat. This day was so exciting, and truly one of the best Father's Day celebrations for us, which

Casandra Johnson

I will forever cherish!

HONOR YOUR FATHER AND MOTHER

Honor thy father and thy mother that thy days may be long upon the land which the LORD thy God giveth thee.

Exodus 20:12

The Bible commands us to honor our father and mother, which is the first commandment with promise.

In June 2006, our family would come together in Atlanta, GA at the Omni Hotel at CNN Center. It would be for the Inaugural Conference and Celebration for Kingdom Journey Enterprises, as well as the official release event for my 1st book "Free to Live Again." This was an exciting time that would span over a two day period. While I knew that daddy could not make the 1st day, I looked forward to his arrival on the 2nd day, which was Saturday, July 1, 2006.

Daddy had to work the night before and told me that he would get on the highway after his shift had ended. This was truly a special day.

Something happened on that day, as I would hear so clearly from my Heavenly Father to publicly honor my natural father during this special occasion. Little did I know that this would be the last opportunity that I would have to publicly pay honor and tribute to daddy in his presence.

As daddy entered the room, on that day, I was honored to call him my father and he was honored to call me his daughter. It was a grand occasion, as our family, including both mama and daddy, were all together in one room. Daddy traveled over 600 miles to Atlanta to speak blessings and affirmation to his "little girls," as this was a family affair. It was a moment that I will never forget, which also caused our relationship to go to a whole new dimension. My life was forever changed as there was an exchange which occurred that I had longed for since the time I was a little girl.

Casandra Johnson

THE BOND – AS IT IS IN THE SPIRIT

Although daddy and I have had a relationship to some degree since the time that I was a little girl, something happened in later years after I became an adult, which was unlike the ordinary. After the conference, our relationship would begin to grow to a level that was beyond the norm. It represented something that I had always longed for. We would now begin to develop a bond that would start to become aligned according to what God ordained for fathers and children, from both a natural and spiritual perspective.

I can recall having a conversation with daddy in July 2007, where it was as if God Himself were speaking through him to me. This in fact had never happened before. The bond was real, it was genuine – He was my daddy and I was his little girl, at the age of 38.

Casandra Johnson

Section 3 – Fast Forward

THE GATHERING

The day was Saturday, September 1, 2007 – Daddy's sister's home was the place. You see, daddy's sister, who is also my godmother, had been diagnosed with stomach cancer just a few months earlier. The doctors had said it was terminal. Just a few weeks prior, she had been in the hospital and the doctors did not expect for her to return home. But she defied the odds!

My daughter and I were moving to Atlanta on the following Monday. We gathered at my aunt's home, where it was also my daughter, daddy's sister and one of his brothers and several family friends.

Whatever it took, I knew that I had to see daddy before I left. Daddy had been going to his sister's house quite frequently to make sure that she was alright and to also take her back and forth to the doctors for appointments and treatments. Daddy had even talked about retiring so that he could be there with his sister.

Daddy's work schedule required him to work all night and he would go to see her during the day. He shared with me that he was starting to get a little tired from working and wanted to be there to help his sister all the time.

Daddy requested family medical leave, which we later learned had been denied because he was not considered to be a "next of kin" by the defined standards of the Family Medical Leave Act. Daddy was his sister's only sibling that lived in the area, and she also had no natural children. His request for the family leave act had been denied, which created a dilemma. He was advised by his employer to use his vacation leave, which he did. On "that day," he was just returning to work for the first time after being out for six weeks. Daddy was planning to resume the routine of working all night, being with his sister during the day, and also continuing to keep up with his lawn business. As circumstances would now have it, he was unable to go back to work anyway, which makes me wonder what his employer ended up doing as a result of him being unable to return to work after all. Strangely enough, as I was finalizing this manuscript, I met a young man all the way in Atlanta who had just received a job offer for the same organization in DC that daddy worked for, and the same type of position. Perhaps he was daddy's replacement after almost a full year.

So the day of our gathering was sort of like a reunion for those of us who were gathered. Again, we laughed, smiled, hugged, ate, and shared cake from one of my aunt's closest friends. This was a time for family, fun, and fellowship. Daddy and I continued to build our bond until we both had to leave. Daddy wished us well, also telling me to make sure that I had enough rest before traveling. He made sure to give my daughter and I one of those firm hugs and also provided us with a gift to help with travel expenses. He gave his blessings and well wishes as we moved forward.

THE FINAL CALL

Daddy would often call to check on us once we moved to Atlanta, to make sure that we were ok and had what we needed. We would often play phone tag, but eventually connect with each other. We had gotten into a ritual of calling on most Saturdays and during the evenings. You see, our journey had not been an easy one, which daddy had known. As we were talking during the final call, he was also getting ready to head out to see about one of his clients - off to do lawns. His parting words during that conversation were "I have to go, but I'll get back to you to help all with what you need to be ok." Remember, daddy didn't live with us when we were growing up and there were in fact times when we didn't have everything that we needed. In later years however, daddy tried to do everything possible to ensure that his children and grandchildren were taken care of.

Casandra Johnson

"THAT DAY"

On Sunday, October 14, 2007, I attended service at New Birth Missionary Baptist Church where Bishop Eddie Long is the senior pastor. Prior to the end of service, Elder Bernice King, daughter of the late Dr. Martin Luther King, Jr. was invited to the podium to share remarks with the congregation. We had just recently moved to Atlanta and were visiting New Birth on that day.

I had told daddy during our last conversation that I had recently met Bernice King. She was in fact one of the very first people to personally greet me with "Welcome to Atlanta!"

There was so much that was very special about that day. It was the opening weekend for Tyler Perry's movie "Why Did I Get Married," which Bishop Long took a moment to acknowledge Tyler Perry's attendance at the service and thank everyone for helping to make it number one at the box office. Just a couple of weeks prior, I had the privilege of attending the pre-screening for the movie and the studio taping with Tyler Perry for his talk show, which also included the cast from the movie.

As I watched the pre-screening and also sat in the studio during the taping, even staying back afterwards talking with the cast and producer, Mr. Ruben Cannon, I continued to think about Tyler Perry's previous movie, "Daddy's Little Girls." The movie was centered around a father and three little girls, who were actually natural sisters. I just couldn't shake it, and even during worship service when Bishop Long made the announcement, "Daddy's Little Girls" continued to remain at the forefront of my mind. This proved to be a landmark day where so much stood out to me during the service as it relates to fathers and their little girls.

As Elder Bernice King began to speak, she went on to quote words from one of her daddy's most famous speeches "I Have A Dream." There was something that illuminated in the atmosphere when she echoed words spoken by her father. It caused me to immediately reflect on a statement that my father had recently made to me as it related to our transition to Atlanta. My father had stated that he believed that God was sending us to Atlanta and that he knew that it was in my heart to be where God was sending me. He said "I may not live to see you get there, but I know that you will get there." Something happened for me when Elder King uttered similar words spoken by her father during his speech. You see my daddy came in 2006 for the conference and was able to see a glimpse of what was to come. He also saw us off right before we left to move to Atlanta. There were so many plans even to the extent of daddy saying that he wanted to get in his car and drive back to Atlanta to visit us.

Just a few hours after leaving service, the lives of daddy's "three little girls" were forever changed.

Daddy's Gone

Daddy had been outside in front of his home, working on his truck. This was nothing unusual, as it was what he would often do because he was good at it. This time however, something went terribly wrong. As a result, there was a loud noise which prompted one of the neighbors to come running outside.

Daddy lived alone, but was known as one of the neighborhood icons or legends. He could often be found in the community serving and helping his fellow neighbors. On "that day" however, the neighbors would have to come to daddy's rescue to aid, comfort and take care of him during his time of need.

When the neighbor who heard the noise came out, he found daddy sitting on the lawn, apparently in a lot of pain, with his cell phone in hand. By this time, daddy had called 9-1-1, the very same number for which he was once a first responder.

When the neighbor noticed daddy's phone in his hand, he asked "Is there anyone else that I can call for you?"

Daddy responded with "Call my oldest daughter."

This led the neighbor to begin looking for his oldest daughter's name, Sharon, in the cell phone directory.

Daddy would say "No, it's not under her name, it's under "1st Born"." Thus a new era would begin!

Daddy's little girls were the first three numbers in his cell phone directory, listed as "1st Born", "2nd Born", and "3rd Born".

When "1st Born" was notified, it was like de ja vu. The series of events would be similar to what we had experienced just a few years before. Phone calls would begin going out to the family members. We would in turn begin calling on the God of our salvation. "1st Born" and "3rd Born" would set in motion to get on the clear highway during the late hours of the night enroute to the hospital. In just a few hours, this same highway would become congested with thousands of commuters who would be going to work. Once again, they were headed to another hospital that is known around the country for having one of the leading shock trauma units.

The difference this time however "2nd Born" was was over 600 miles away. The only thing that I could do at that particular moment was pray and remain near the phone for any updates. My mindset however was that daddy would be ok. My thoughts at that time were if I needed to go home, it may just be for the purpose of providing assistance to daddy as he recovered.

Section 3 – Fast Forward

Just hours prior to this phone call, I had received a call from mama shortly after church. She shared with me that she had experienced some excruciating chest pains that came from out of nowhere. She stated that it felt like something had crushed her chest and she prayed to God that she would not die like this. She in turn laid down on her bed and the pain went away shortly thereafter. Although mama and daddy had been divorced for close to 30 years, what she was in fact feeling was the pain that he would soon experience.

Upon arriving at the hospital, 1st Born and 3rd Born would sit in the waiting room. This time was a little different from their past experience though. Daddy had been air-lifted to the hospital by med-evac, however he was already in the operating room undergoing surgery by the time they arrived. They were not able to see him or find out from the doctors what was going on. Everyone had the same thoughts however - that daddy had been injured, was being treated, and that he would be ok. Remember, we had been "here" before!

After several hours of surgery, the doctors would come out for the first time at approximately 4:00 in the morning to notify "1st Born" and "3rd Born" that they could not stop the bleeding, but they would continue to try. They would in turn call mama to relay the news, who would call "2nd Born".

As "2nd Born" sat on the other end of the phone, some 600 miles away, the only apparent thoughts that came to mind were "Many people have been hit by a vehicle, and they were ok, so of course he would be ok too. "

"But why wouldn't the bleeding stop? Why certainly they had the best physicians working on him. "

Within the same hour, one of the most devastating events would occur. The hospital staff would come out of the operating room to notify "1st Born" and "3rd Born" that they had done all they could do, but daddy did not make it.

They would now stand in the hospital, grieving as daddy's spirit would transition from his lifeless body into eternity; Not having the opportunity to speak to him one last time. A few minutes later, they would find themselves standing together in the hospital room with daddy's lifeless body, with "3rd Born" noticing a tear in one of his eyes.

And 2nd Born would be notified by a phone call from mama. Upon hearing the news, my instant reaction was to push the "end" button on the phone and scream." The call was immediately disconnected. For that particular moment, it was literally as if my world had also just ended - like a piece of me had just been disconnected.

Our daddy was gone, suddenly. Daddy was gone - not from an illness or as a result of something that was expected, but manner of death - an accident; cause of death - crushing injuries to the torso.

I would now have to prepare to go home to meet daddy - not for crabs, or pizza,

Casandra Johnson

or McDonalds, or for fun and fellowship, but for the tremendous task of making plans to honor daddy and ensure that he had the proper burial.

How could it be?

God tell me this wasn't so.

Was I dreaming?

When would I wake up?

What were we to do?

Because of the memories created over a time span of 43 years, these same three girls would rise to the occasion to begin making final arrangements that would allow us to remember, honor and pay tribute to daddy, and give him the proper burial that was fitting for a soldier gone home. On "that day," our ages were 43, 38, and 35 respectively, each with children of our own, but still daddy's little girls.

THE ULTIMATE CALL

After receiving the final call, the challenge that I now faced was the fulfillment of the Ultimate Call, which was one that had come with a great degree of opposition. It was in fact the one that God would use daddy to affirm for his little girl prior to his transition.

The response to this call was certainly nothing that I could do in and of myself because it had been a difficult road in preparing for that day. Even up until the time of the service, a moment of great opposition came where daddy's little girl wanted to walk away and go and sit with the rest of the family as a result of pain brought that I had become all too familiar with, but with a certainty that God had called me. To my two sisters in Christ who would understand the challenge and also stood with me on that day, I can't thank you enough for being there!

The challenges that I would face was something that daddy knew before his passing. Daddy would in fact be there to help me to move forward based on who God said that I was and who God allowed him to confirm as my daddy. It was imperative for me to respond to "The Ultimate Call" on that day that my Heavenly Father had ordained for me to answer before the beginning of time. It was certainly nothing that I could do in and of myself, but I had to trust God to be able to stand. What would help me was God allowing me to block out the negative voices and instead, continue hearing my daddy's voice, saying just as if God Himself were speaking, "I believe in what God has called you to do."

So on this day, daddy's three little girls rose to the occasion to celebrate his life. We stood on that day with his obituary in hand displaying a photo of daddy that would be most fitting and significant. What I saw was daddy tipping his hat off to us, which symbolized him telling us – you are my little girls, I believe in you, go forward and do what God has created you to do.

So as people wondered and asked how I could stand and deliver daddy's eulogy during one of the most difficult moments of my life, it was because of my Heavenly Father and the Bond that He allowed me to develop with my natural father. Our relationship had become solid and I was at peace. I can honestly say that while I grieve because of the loss, we were however able to share so much prior to his passing where I didn't feel like anything was left undone, or words left unspoken that I wish that I could have shared with him before he passed. The development of a bond with daddy was critical to me as an adult as well as for him. It was a relationship that was worth building, where we both did everything within our power and by the strength and grace of God to ensure that our relationship was solid.

When daddy passed away and even during his home going celebration, I realized that grieving was normal, as even "Jesus wept" as reflected in John

11:35 as a result of the loss of his friend, Lazarus. But there is also another passage of scripture in Psalms 30:5 that I find great comfort in which states "Weeping may endure for a night, but joy cometh in the morning." Guess what, it's morning!

I miss daddy and often think about him and the fact that he's no longer with us here on Earth. Although his passing was a sudden and tragic one, I do have peace because of the bond that we developed, the conversations that we shared, and the events that God allowed him to witness in my life. He was my daddy and at 38 years old, I was still his little girl. We laughed together, we joked together, we hugged each other, we shared stories, I told him I loved him and he told me he loved me too. He affirmed me and told me he believed in what God had called me to do. This was so important.

What we learned in our adult years was that while daddy was not in the home with us as little girls growing up, he did love and believe in his little girls. In turn, he also left a legacy and we found it important to pick up the mantle and continue moving forward.

HONORING DADDY'S FINAL REQUEST

During daddy's final days, he would relay his admiration for Psalms 23 to his little girls, which reads as follows:

"The LORD is my Shepherd; I shall not want.

He maketh me to lie down in green pastures: He leadeth me beside the still waters.

He restoreth my soul: He leadeth me in the paths of righteousness for His name's sake.

Yea, though I walk through the valley of the shadow of death, I will fear no evil: for thou art with me; thy rod and thy staff, they comfort me.

Thou preparest a table before me in the presence of mine enemies: thou anointest my head with oil; my cup runneth over.

Surely goodness and mercy shall follow me all of the days of my life: and I will dwell in the house of the LORD forever."

In July 2007, daddy and I had an intense conversation centered around the 23rd Psalms. During his last conversation with "1st Born", which was the Friday before he passed, he also shared that he wanted the 23rd Psalms sang at his funeral. Little did either of us know that the time would soon come. In honor of one of his final requests, the 23rd Psalms became the central theme for daddy's home going celebration.

During my conversation with daddy, we discussed and meditated on the entire passage of scripture. Our discussion went something like this:

You see, daddy understood that there was a stage of his journey that he could not travel alone, even though he may have thought differently during earlier years of his life. For this stage of the journey, he knew that he would need the Lord as the Shepherd of his soul to lead and guide him. What he told me was Casandra, as you go forward to do what God has called you to do, make sure that you let God lead and guide you, and do not attempt to do anything in and of yourself. He stated that there were a lot of people doing "stuff" but there were questions as to whether they were all truly being led by the Lord and following his instructions and directions. He stated that in ministry, God has to lead you and that it was imperative that you follow his every command because this walk would not be easy, but He would in fact provide everything that you needed. He went on to say that in following Him, He would lead you beside green pastures and still waters. There would be blessings that He would bestow upon you, He would lead you to do what was right for His name's sake and it was imperative that you followed the right path. Daddy went on to state that but on this walk, it would not always be easy. He got stirred up when he got to the point of speaking of the valley experiences. He stopped and emphasized that when you get to that point, remember that although there would be valley experiences, you do not stay there, but you walk through it and as you are going through it that God would always be there to comfort you. Daddy admonished me to not be afraid of the evil that would attempt to come against me during those valley experiences because it was only temporary, and it was certain that God would always be with me.

Just as God allowed me to share this while delivering daddy's eulogy, I believe that daddy was also prophesying to himself during our conversation as it relates to what was to come. During that very difficult moment of his life, not only was God there with daddy during his final hours, but he also sent angels in the form of his neighbors, as well as a young police officer, one of Prince George's finest. Daddy's career as a police officer was truly one of his 1st loves and amazingly enough, it would be a police officer that God would send to be with him and comfort him during his final moments in this life. As God allowed me to go on and share during the service, the part where I in turn got excited was the passage of the 23rd Psalms that God prepared a table in the presence of his enemies and anointed his head with oil and allowed his cup to run over. It was at this point that the enemy had to let go and come into realization and subjection that he could not have daddy, but God's hand was in fact upon him as He snatched him away from the hand of the enemy. All that the enemy could do at that point was sit back and watch in defeat as God led daddy home to safety.

NEVER WOULD HAVE MADE IT

As people wondered how, the only thing that truly allowed us to make it on that day was the grace of God. Without Him, my sisters and I never would have made it and it is in Him that we trust to continue to guide us forward. My father has left a legacy even from his final resting place, where his tombstone inscription reads "In God We Trust."

Daddy's funeral was on October 23, 2007. Who would have known that exactly 3 months after this date, I would find myself sitting in the funeral of two young police officers from DeKalb County Georgia who were violently gunned down while in the line of duty. Ironically enough, I had received an invitation to attend another studio taping for Tyler Perry's movie that was being recorded on the same day, which many people would have dreamed of attending. There was however something within me that had to go and honor these two young officers, who had both left behind spouses and young children. As I attended the service at New Birth, and sat amongst thousands of police officers who had traveled from near and far to pay their final respect to their fallen comrades, I felt as though I was sitting in to represent my daddy, one of Washington, DC's finest.

Casandra Johnson

Section 4 - A Tribute To Daddy

Casandra Johnson

DADDY MADE THE DIFFERENCE

Prior to daddy's passing, I went through a very difficult period in my life where I found myself in a place that I never would have imagined. Mama was there, as always with her prayers, encouragement, love, and support, just as she always had been. But I was still having a difficult time as a result of events that would crush my heart and cause me to retreat and often sit in a room, paralyzed. I struggled, and cried, not knowing what to do for a long time. When I finally got the courage to call daddy, he came along and made the difference - As it is in the spirit, so it is in the natural.

I clearly remember when and how it happened. When my daddy came along and affirmed me, it was if there was a new me. I stood tall, held my head up, and once again found the belief in who God said that I was based on the words spoken into my life by daddy.

So many times, little girls will seek love and affirmation from different places, when what they are really searching for is love and affirmation from daddy. As a result, they often find themselves hurt, in so much pain, and it becomes constant to the point where they may wonder if the cycle will ever end. Indeed, we do want the cycle of pain to end. Our Heavenly Father has given our earthly daddy the power to speak into the lives of his little girls and boys in order to make a difference.

When daddy speaks and affirms who you are, there's nothing that anyone can do to make you believe any different. Little girls, remember that daddy gave you your name and that doesn't change until he releases it to be so. Don't let anyone else go naming you and calling you something that you are not, to the point that you believe it and begin to die inside. That's where I was. I started to literally die inside and while mama was there to love, nurture and encourage me, when daddy came along to speak into my life and affirm me, he made the difference. At the time when he spoke and told me, "I believe in you," that's when there was a change in my life and I began to take the necessary steps to really move forward into who God had called me to be. Daddy spoke and gave life - just as he did to bring me into this world and also give me my name. But it seemed like just as quickly as it happened, daddy was gone - suddenly. For a brief period of time, I found myself wanting to retreat once again and wondering "why" at this stage of my journey. It was at this point that my Heavenly Father spoke and said I have created you and you are fearfully and wonderfully made. There were several scriptures of affirmation that I was also reminded of at that time:

> *"No one will be able to stand against you all the days of your life. As I was with Moses, so I will be with you; I will never leave you nor forsake you." Joshua 1:5 NIV*

Casandra Johnson

> "Before I formed thee in the belly I knew thee, and before thou camest forth out of the wound I sanctified thee, and I ordained thee a prophet unto the nations." Jeremiah 1:5

> "For I know the thoughts that I think towards you, saith the Lord, thoughts of peace, and not of evil, to give you an expected end." Jeremiah 29:11

For everyone that has never received words of affirmation from your natural father, whether they are still alive or have passed, today, please allow me to share and impart these words into your life that my daddy shared with me:

> "I believe in who God has created you to be!"

> "Know that the world has been forever changed because YOU are here!"

> "Move Forward and be all that God has created you to be and Enjoy the Journey!"

Yes, mama made the difference, but daddy certainly did too!

SECTION 5 – THE JOURNEY HOME

As I have the privilege of speaking with different people on a day-to-day basis, I often take the time to ask the following questions:

- Who Are You?
- Where Are You Going?
- Are You There Yet?

While these may sound like very basic questions, I submit to you that they are very important for anyone who truly has a desire to move forward and live their life to the fullest! I would like to share a story, which will explain why I believe these questions are important for one to understand.

Throughout my life's journey, I have had the privilege of traveling to many locations across the United States, and to several foreign nations. Because of my travels, I have been afforded with the opportunity to meet and be in the company of many great people, some of whom others only dream of meeting. In July 2008, I had the honor of taking "the journey home" to a small town called Port Gibson, MS, which is the area where both of my parents were born and raised. On this particular weekend, many people who represented several generations traveled from all over the United States to attend our family reunion. This was in fact the first that I have had the opportunity of attending with this group of family members in close to 30 years. What we learned in our "journey home" was this was actually the first time that many of our relatives from the existing generations had ever traveled to Port Gibson to see where and how their parents and forefathers were raised. I must admit that at that time, I was 39 years old and this was only my second visit to Port Gibson, and the first for my daughter.

In March 1968, my parents headed "north" to Washington, DC, arriving just one month before the assassination of Dr. Martin Luther King, Jr., where they witnessed firsthand the riots and destruction that occurred throughout the city. Many of their other relatives also migrated to various locations throughout the United States in an effort to raise their own families in an environment that was different from what they had once known in Port Gibson. As we had the opportunity to tour the different areas of Port Gibson, which has not changed very much from the time that our parents were raised there in the 40s, 50s, and 60s, many of us were able to come to several realizations that aided us with discovering more about who we were based on the background and experiences of our parents and forefathers. My grandparents had been very active in Mississippi during the Civil Rights Movement and my parents were products of

Casandra Johnson

the segregated school systems and public facilities, which meant that I was in fact just one generation removed from this era. I actually did not even realize this until I was in my early 20s. Many other family members were not even aware of some of the critical roles that their family members had during this era and the danger that they faced as a result of events that occurred.

As this particular journey came to an end, I sat in total awe as I reflected on all that occurred over the course of this 3-day period. What I can tell you is that of all the places that I have traveled and the many people whom I have been honored to meet, this particular trip proved to be one of the most profound and life changing moments of my life, ever. It was during this trip where I had the opportunity to meet some of the greatest people in the world, which was my family!

My father recently passed away as a result of injuries sustained in a tragic accident. This particular journey to Port Gibson served as an opportunity for me to reconnect with who he was, as well as make a greater connection with my mother, who I had the honor of traveling to Port Gibson with and hearing her share stories firsthand about our family history. This is something that so many people have gotten far away from and in essence, it makes it very difficult to make the connection with who you really are. In turn, I submit that it creates an even greater difficulty in knowing where you are going.

Today, I would like challenge you with the following questions:

- Has your family come together for a family reunion within the past five years? This does not include a wedding or funeral, but a real family reunion.
- Have you ever visited the location where your parents were born or re-visited the location where you were actually born if you no longer live there? If you have children, have you ever taken them to these locations?
- Have you recently taken the time to call or visit an older family member to just talk, share and learn from them?

If you answered no to any of these questions, I encourage you to begin making plans and take action to do what may actually turn out to be one of the most significant experiences of your life.

If you answered yes to these questions, I celebrate you and encourage you to keep it going in order to continue creating a lasting impact for future generations!

SECTION 6 – DEAR DADDY: AN ANTHOLOGY OF TRIBUTES, NOTES, AND MEMORABLE MOMENTS

Casandra Johnson

DEDICATION FROM IKE JOHNSON'S LITTLE GIRLS

We know you left us suddenly
But you gave us so many years of joy
You passed on your wisdom and knowledge
And made us promise to never forget

You wanted to make sure we were happy
And you wouldn't accept anything less
Each and every time we saw each other
Your keen words would be at best

You always said never boast on yourself
But let others boast about you
Come to find out Daddy, everybody knew about us
Because of your never ending boast

Daddy, our lives will not end without you
Because you are part of us
But now it's our time to boast
About the father who saw us through

We love you Daddy and we miss you
And you said if there was anything you can do
Just keep on guiding us Daddy
With all the memories of you

Sharon, Casandra, and Stephanie

Casandra Johnson

TRIBUTE TO DADDY FROM SHARON ANN BOYDE - "1ST BORN"

When I woke up this morning the first thing I did was get my printed, draft copy from the computer of "Dear Daddy". I just read the book. Of course I was very happy with what I read but I'm also in tears. It's been almost a year since the telephone call that daddy had been injured and subsequently died the next morning. It's still so fresh in my mind as though it was just yesterday.
We often wonder when the grieving process ends when a parent passes away but I'm coming to realize that it doesn't end because as children we will always long for the conversation, wisdom, and guidance. But the one thing that I am so grateful for is that the memories of those conversations, wisdom, and guidance will always be there in our hearts, mind, and soul. We get to the point that we know that daddy's physical body is not here but he will always live within us. We will always be able to build on what he taught us. The memories that we have with him will always be there. The one statement that rings out from Daddy to me is that he told me that we will never be able to understand why certain circumstances happens in our lives but you must keep trusting God. Whatever you do don't you ever stop trusting God. "In God We Trust". Daddy's words are the words that help me get thru his death. It's not up to me to understand why it happened the way it did but I trust God. I have to trust God.

MEMORABLE MOMENTS OF A DAUGHTER GROWING UP IN THE SOUTH – LOVINGLY SUBMITTED BY RUTH HALL

Daddy John owned a farm in the southern parts of Georgia. I have countless memories of him sloshing through springtime rain; dodging balls of hail as he planted his crops. The summer months found him toiling under the scorching sun tending to tender shoots. In the fall he struggled to reap the harvest of his labor and winter brought fierce cold winds to beat against his veneer. Daddy traded his struggles for his heavenly inheritance, leaving a quality life for his offspring to enjoy. Everyday I thank God for the man who introduced me to Jesus. And for epitomizing, in our home, the scripture recorded in Joshua 24:15.

After having to leave school at an early age to financially care for his mother and sisters, I'm sure life was hard for him. He probably made many mistakes. But the word of God guarantees the race is given to the ones who endure to the end. I was indeed fortunate to have witnessed the finished product. Daddy did not compromise his life. Nor did he water down his walk with God. He lived an upright life before God. A life I strive to match or surpass daily.

Casandra Johnson

MEMORABLE MOMENTS FROM BRENDA JENKINS

My most memorable moments with my Dad were the many times that he called me special, smart and strong. He was my protector. Even though I was raised by my mom, my father' presence was always with me. His visits were special because he made me feel special.

Thank you Daddy, for giving me the perspective, that I am somebody and that I am capable of achievement. Thank you for providing the invisible shield that I would be all right regardless of my fears. I believed that you would take care of all my fears.

In 1980 when you died that belief lingered. In 1991 when I accepted Jesus as my Lord and Savior the protections begin to pass from you to him.

As my relationship grew with Jesus I realize your protection was transferred to my heavenly father. My protection and who I am are all tied up with my heavenly father. I know now that your purpose was to provide protection until I knew for myself about my heavenly father. Thank you, Dad.

MEMORABLE MOMENTS OF JOHN WESLEY BARNES, SR. FROM MS. DORIS WALLS

My best memory of daddy is when I saw him before he passed away. The last thing he said to me is that he loved mama. He said I loved mama baby. I told him that I knew that.

Casandra Johnson

A Tribute To My Father By Ms. Renee Wiggins

My father was there for us always, you never heard
him grumble, cuss or fuss.

He was a quiet strong man. I said this at his funeral.

On May 22, 1922, Ethel and Ned Wiggins, was bestowed a male child and they named him Samuel C. Wiggins - Samuel from the bible was a prophet; a trusted prophet under the teaching of Elijah. Samuel learned
to serve the Lord.

On August 6, 2006, my father was called home.

Our Father, who art in heaven. Samuel Carl Wiggins was his name. Some people have to create a name, my father lived up to his name. He wasn't a prophet but he was given the stewardship to serve and indeed he served mankind.

Thanks Dad,
From your (2) Daughters, 2- grandchildren and 2-great grandchildren.

Section 6 – Dear Daddy: An Anthology Of Tributes, Notes, And Memorable Moments

MEMORABLE MOMENTS WITH MY FATHER BY MS. VICKIE L. EVANS

As a child, I have many fond memories of my father, Robert Ellis! I was "Daddy's Little Girl"; not to mention, I was raised as an only child. My Dad and I were inseparable. He would carry me on his shoulders until I became too heavy to carry. I was almost grown before he stopped cutting my pancakes for me (smile). I remember one incident when I was around 4 or 5 years old, my Dad took me to an auto part store and left me in our car (it had to be a 60 model Oldsmobile or something), with the car running. My curiosity got the best of me and I reached over to the driver side and shifted the gears. The car begins to proceed down the hill at a rapid pace. You should have seen my Dad chase that car down; and you thought Jessie Owens was the fastest sprinter! My Dad has always been my Protector, my Advocate (he kept my mother off of me many days), and my Guardian Angel (watching over me when times were tough). Although I love my Mother dearly, I am still "Daddy's Little Girl"!

Vickie L. Evans is the author of The Art of Forgiving, and Know Your Worth! (Overcoming the Dragon of Low Self-Esteem). She is the producer and playwright of the hit gospel stage play A Change Is Gonna Come, and the President of her own talent promotion agency, Soaring High Productions.

Casandra Johnson

My Most Memorable Moments Of My Granddaddy, John Wesley Barnes, Sr.

I have so many fond memories of my grandfather.

Our granddaddy truly believed in family. He would stress all the time that family was the most important people to a person. Being the oldest grandchild and for a period of time living with my mother and grandparents, he was always there for my mother.

When the grandchildren all went to Mississippi to visit our grandparents, I had my own special day with my granddad as the oldest grandchild. We would drive down the highway and visit the hospital where I was born. He would take me to see the doctor who   helped me with my bronchitis attacks. After visiting a few people, I knew what was next – Dairy Queen. We ordered a vanilla ice cream cone dipped in chocolate. We sat on the bench to eat our ice cream. Of course, before you knew it, I would have ice cream all down my hands and arm. Granddaddy got some napkins and cleaned me up. I'm sorry to my sisters and cousins, but this was my special day and we couldn't come back with evidence. Whenever I go to Dairy Queen, I still order my vanilla ice cream cone dipped in chocolate. Granddaddy I miss you so much. You showed all of your grandchildren unconditional love. We miss your kisses.

Sharon Ann Boyde, 1st Born Grandchild

THOUGHTS OF MY DAD – BY MS. TONYA Y. VANFIELD

My heart was moved to prayer when I was first requested to briefly elaborate my most memorable thought respecting my father (who had recently passed away). The Lord spoke to me swiftly, "Honor your father and your mother, that your days may be long upon the land which the LORD your God is giving you." That being said, loudly and clearly, I believe there is one word which would prepare the reader for what I am about to say…"enigmatic." As was mentioned at his funeral service, for those who knew him, those individuals knew that he was a man who truly spoke for himself. For those who were in attendance at his service out of love and compassion for the family, but who never really got to know him, there are no words to adequately describe him. However, as a father, his strength of character and example of what it meant to "be a man" will live in the hearts and minds of my brother and myself until we depart this life for a better one. This was a man who had little to give, but on the other hand gave everything because he gave of himself. To his family first, his career, his friends, and to his neighbors, he gave. As for the man in the streets – either the beggar or the thief, he had two separate philosophies: he would not willingly allow anything to be taken from him by force nor violence, but out of compassion and love for another human being, would give the shirt off of his back – if asked. There is no one particular thought which comes to mind concerning him. A complicated man, yet very straight-forward. You always knew where he stood on any issue. He was a man of dignity, honor, strength and courage. His latter days were wrought with pain and physical suffering. However, I am reminded of the Word of God says "Therefore, since Christ suffered for us in the flesh, arm yourselves also with the same mind, for he who has suffered in the flesh has ceased from sin.[1] My dad has gone home to be with the Lord. Even as I viewed his remains, so peaceful there, so dignified looking, he was glorifying God. My grief has been transformed into abundant joy knowing that now my father is taking a well-deserved rest, in the arms of our Lord and Savior Jesus Christ. Until we meet again, love, Tonya.

---

[1] I Peter 4:1

Casandra Johnson

MY MOST MEMORABLE MOMENT BY MS. DONNA COURSEY

At a time when my father is very sick, and holding on by the prayers of the righteous, the time I am most grateful for is the day my father said to me " Donna, you are a Coursey and we believe Jesus to be the Son of God". During this time I was a practicing Muslim, a very rebellious teenager, and a prominent speaker for the "Black Power" movement. That conversation would always come to my mind and invade my thoughts. I accepted Christ at the age of 21, and have never thought twice about who Jesus is. I may have had some twists and turns, but thank God for Jesus and my father.

Section 6 – Dear Daddy: An Anthology Of Tributes, Notes, And Memorable Moments

MEMORABLE MOMENTS BY MS. CLAIRE TIMMS

The first is that when I was a teenager, my parents divorced in order to keep our sanity due to the demons my mother was fighting. My dad fought for and got custody of his 2 children and did his best to raise us. So as an acknowledgement of his hard work, I would give him Mother's Day cards on Mother's Day!!

The other story is about when I had thyroid cancer surgery. I will never forget waking up in my hospital room all hooked up to the tubes and wires. And there was my father standing next to my bed, sobbing. This rough, tough as nails man had a soft side and for the first time in my life, I saw that he was afraid! And for the first time in my life, it was me telling my dad that everything was going to be all right!!

Casandra Johnson

Tribute To My Father By Major Timothy O. Evans, USMC (Ret.)

I would like to share the words my father wrote in my Bible to me upon giving it to me:

The Bible contains the mind of God, the state of man, the way of salvation, the doom of sinners, and the happiness of believers. It's doctrines are holy, it's precepts are binding, it's histories are true, and it's decisions are immutable. Read it to be wise, believe it to be safe, and practice it to be holy. It contains light to direct you, food to support you, and comfort to cheer you.

It is the traveler's map, the pilgrim's staff, the pilots compass, the soldier's sword, and the Christian's charter. Here paradise is restored, Heaven opened, and the gates of hell disclosed.

My answered prayer has come to pass that you my son would be given this same hunger and thirst for God as I have. My love and prayers always.

Your Pops

A Tribute To My Father, John Wesley Barnes, Sr. From Lizzie Marie Johnson

My Father was a man of integrity and character. Ever since I can remember him as a little girl, he always had an attribute of love for his family and other people. He told us about his mother dying when he was young and had two siblings, Luther and Marie, and they were raised by his grandmother Lizzie, who he adored. He named me after his grandmother and sister and I was always teased because my Siblings' stated all the time you are just like your father but I want to take that today as a compliment. I wouldn't trade him for any other father in the world because he was always there for us.

He taught us to be thankful for what we had, disciplined us and raised us in a Christian home. He loved my mother and took care of her. I want to say Father Thank You.

SECTION 7 - PREPARING FOR WHAT IS CERTAIN

To everything there is a season, and a time to every purpose under the heaven: A time to be born, and a time to die; a time to plan, and a time to pluck up that which is planted; Ecclesiastes 3:1-2

Death is certain, and it's very important to prepare and set plans in motion so that your loved ones don't have to experience the unnecessary pain that has become the norm for many families during the time of passing of a loved one. My mother's parents prepared so that their children would not have to experience these struggles. My grandparents had eight children who reached adulthood before their parents passed away. When their mama and daddy passed away, all they had to do was simply show up because everything was set in motion. When grandma died suddenly at the young age of 52, granddaddy was the next of kin. He made the decisions, took care of everything, and their adult children simply showed up and fell in line. For years, I asked God why he took my grandma first and at such a young age. As I grew older, I understood a little more. It was almost 15 years later before granddaddy passed away, but the same was the case. Granddaddy had remarried, but he made sure that the arrangements were set and all the details of what he wanted were known, so once again, the same eight children simply showed up.

Now here stood three of their granddaughters in October 2007, being faced with having to make difficult decisions as a result of daddy's sudden passing. Daddy was not married when he passed, so we were the next of kin and had the responsibility of planning his final arrangements as a result of daddy not having a written will in place. What we learned was that daddy was scheduled to meet with an attorney on the day that he passed in order to begin the process of preparing a will. In the absence of a will, in so many cases, all that one has to go on is what they believe one may have desired based on discussions and hearsay, and documents that can be readily accessed.

Although daddy didn't have a will, his three girls were able to go into his home and locate several documents that provided key information to help us with the decision making, in addition to what we knew to be our daddy's desires based on conversations with him. After the funeral, when daddy's little girls showed up at the attorney's office to start the probate process, we were told that we were in much better shape than most clients in a situation like this, especially considering that none of us lived in daddy's home.

Because death is certain and something that we must all encounter, here are some of the steps that I recommend for every adult to consider based on what daddy's little girls learned.

- First and foremost, prepare a will outlining all of your desires, and file it with the appropriate organizations and individuals.
- Gather all of the supporting documents for the will that deal with assets for your estate and accounts that name beneficiaries.
- Review these documents on an annual basis to ensure that they are up to date and make any necessary revisions, such as beneficiaries. Factor in any events that have occurred during that period to include births, deaths, marriages, and divorces.
- Let trusted sources know where this information is located.
- Designate an Executor/Power of Attorney.
- Identify your last wishes for your funeral services and burial, to include locations and specific desires such as songs or specific individuals that you would like to participate.
- Provide key information for your obituary, or have copies of obituaries of close relatives to help in providing key information about your family.
- Even go to the extent of identifying a suit/dress that you would like to be buried in, along with a photo for your program.

In outlining this key information, it helps to dismiss room for arguments and confusion among spouses, parents, children, and siblings.

Section 7 - Preparing For What Is Certain

KEY LIST OF INFORMATION
(GATHER INFORMATION AND FILL IN THE BLANKS)

Name
Date of Birth
Address
Social Security Number
Next of Kin
Will Yes/No
Location of where will is filed

Spouse's Name
Alive or Deceased
Married or Divorced
Spouse's Address

Spouse's Phone Number

Children's Names
Alive or Deceased
Children's Address

Children's Phone Numbers

Mother's Name
Alive or Deceased
Mother's Address
Mother's Phone Number

Father's Name
Alive or Deceased
Father's Address
Father's Phone Number

# of Siblings
Siblings Names and Phone Numbers

Last Place of Employment
Address
Phone Number
Employee ID #

Life Insurance Policies
Company Name
Amount

Casandra Johnson

Policy #
Address
Phone Number
Beneficiaries Names and Phone Numbers

Accidental Death Insurance Policies
Company Name
Amount
Policy #
Address
Phone Number
Beneficiaries Names and Phone Numbers

Bank Accounts
Bank Name
Account #
Address
Phone Number
Beneficiaries Names and Phone Numbers

Investment Accounts
Company Name
Amount
Account #
Address
Phone Number
Beneficiaries Names and Phone Numbers

Real Estate
Address
Owned or Financed
Finance Company Name
Account Number
Address
Phone Number
Insurance - Yes/No

Vehicles
Make and Model
Owned or Financed
Finance Company Name
Account Number
Address
Phone Number

Section 7 - Preparing For What Is Certain

Insurance - Yes/No

Other Major Assets

Location of Documents
Location of Will
Safe Deposit - Yes/No
Burial or Cremation
Church Name
Funeral Home
Cemetery Name
Cemetery Location
Eulogist
Special Songs
Special Input to Obituary
Photo
Attire

Birth Certificate - Self, Spouse, and Children
Marriage Certificates
Divorce Certificates
Deeds
Titles
Insurance Policies

Casandra Johnson

APPENDIX – THE DASH

DADDY'S OBITUARY

"The Lord is my shepherd, I shall not want. He maketh me to lie down in green pastures: He leadeth me beside the still waters. He restoreth my soul. He leadeth me in the paths of righteousness for His name's sake. Yea, though I walk through the valley of the shadow of death, I will fear no evil: for Thou art with me; thy rod and thy staff they comfort me. Thou preparest a table before me in the presence of mine enemies: thou anointest my head with oil; my cup runneth over. Surely goodness and mercy shall follow me all the days of my life: and I will dwell in the house of the Lord for ever." PSALMS 23

Issac Johnson, Jr. (Ike) was born in Tillman, MS on February 2nd, 1944 to Isaac and Julia Johnson. He departed this life on Monday, October 15th, 2007 at 4:22 a.m. at the Washington Hospital Center in Washington, DC.

Ike attended public schools in Claiborne County, MS, where he played football and graduated from Addison High in 1963. After graduation, he joined the United States Army in 1964 and was stationed in Germany and Texas. He received an honorable discharge in 1967 and moved his family to Washington, DC in 1968. After arriving in Washington, DC, he accepted a position with one of the area's landmark establishments, Woodward and Lothrop. He attended American University where he completed several college courses in Criminal Justice and joined the DC Metropolitan Police Department, where he was assigned to the 3rd District. He was medically retired from the Police Department due to an injury sustained as a result of a heroic act while in the line of duty. At the time of his passing, Ike was employed as a contractor for the U.S. Marshall Service. He also stayed busy doing what he loved by providing services to numerous clients through his landscaping business, Ike's Lawn Service. He was an active member of the Fraternal Order of Police and the John W. Freeman Grand Commandery Knights Templar Prince Hall Affiliation of Washington, DC.

He leaves to cherish his memories a loving mother, Mrs. Julia Johnson of Port Gibson, MS, three daughters, Sharon Boyde of Fredericksburg, VA; Casandra Johnson of Atlanta, GA; and Stephanie Gordon of Dumfries, VA; six grandchildren, Marcus, Michael Christopher, Brittany, Iesha, Shaunice, and Michael Anthony; one great-granddaughter, Daprincia; eight brothers, Edward (Gloria) Johnson of Chicago, IL; Rev. Hugh (Barbara) Johnson, Sr. of Port Gibson, MS; James (Cherrie) Devine of Downers Grove, IL; Elvin (Birdie) Johnson, Ulessiah Johnson, and Charlie Johnson, all of Jackson, MS; Tommy

Casandra Johnson

Johnson of Grambling, LA; and Coney (Eva) Johnson of Port Gibson, MS; six sisters, Annie Carroll of Tillman, MS; Frances Allen of Chicago, IL; Minnie Lee Broadway of Champaign, IL; Georgia Wilson of Washington, DC; Linda Johnson and Geraldine Johnson, both of Port Gibson, MS; four aunts, Sadie Ruth Johnson and Rosetta Johnson, both of Port Gibson, MS; Essie Willis of Atlanta, GA; and Gladys Bowie of Greenwood, MS; one uncle, Samuel Harris of Chicago, IL; and a host of nephews, nieces, other relatives, and friends.

ABOUT THE AUTHOR

Casandra Johnson is the President and Founder of Kingdom Journey Enterprises, a ministry organization which has been created to empower, inspire, equip, and connect leaders for the advancing of God's Kingdom in the Earth. Casandra is a Licensed Minister with a Masters of Arts Degree in Biblical Studies from Beulah Heights University, and she is currently pursuing a Master of Divinity degree. She has traveled extensively and authored and contributed to numerous books, articles, and scholarly research papers. To learn more information or to contact Casandra for speaking engagements or book signings, visit www.casandrajohnson.com.

Casandra Johnson

ABOUT KINGDOM JOURNEY PRESS

Kingdom Journey Press, Inc. is a full-service publishing company specializing in providing customized services to support our clients from the conception of an idea to getting HIStory to the masses! Since the time of inception and in conjunction with our umbrella organization, Kingdom Journey Enterprises, we have become recognized globally for our ability to establish a unique presence, while building relationships with partners and clients consisting of current and aspiring writers, and ministry, business, and community organizations.

Our services include:

- Manuscript Evaluation
- Coaching for current and aspiring authors
- Editing
- Cover and Print Layout Design
- Print and E-Book Format
- Copyright and Distribution
- Marketing and Sales Support

To contact us and to learn more information about our services, we invite you to visit our website at www.kjpressinc.com.

Casandra Johnson

www.ingramcontent.com/pod-product-compliance
Lightning Source LLC
Chambersburg PA
CBHW071721040426
42446CB00011B/2157